Roadmaps to Recovery

A Guided Workbook
for Young People in Treatment

Timothy J. Kahn, M.S.W.

Hi! My name is Buzzbee.
I am your guide. Follow me!

Illustration, Design & Typesetting: Sue Storey, Hinesburg, VT
Editor: Euan Bear
3rd printing: Malloy Incorporated, Ann Arbor, Mi.

ISBN: 1-884444-54-7

$20.00
Bulk discounts available.

Order from:

SaferSocietyPress

P.O. Box 340
Brandon, VT 05733
802-247-3132

Phone orders welcome with Visa or MasterCard.

Hi!

My Name is: _____

My Age is: _____

I started this workbook on: _____

What is in this book?

My Progress Chart

On the next three pages you will keep track of your progress. Color in each car after your counselor has checked your work in each chapter of this book. Your counselor might also give you a sticker after you finish each chapter. With this chart, you can really see how you are doing. Have a great trip through **ROADMAPS** with Buzzbee as your guide!

Buzzbee says, "Color me now, before you start!"

Chapter 1

Chapter 2

Chapter 3

Chapter 4

Chapter 5

Chapter 6

Chapter 7

Chapter 11

Chapter 8

Chapter 12

Chapter 9

Chapter 13

Chapter 10

Chapter 14

Chapter 15

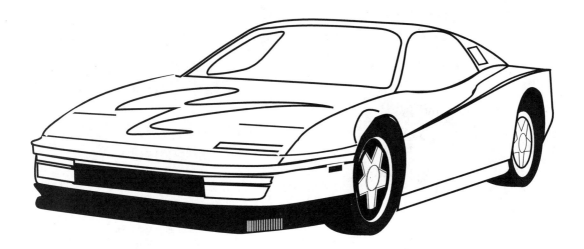

You can decorate this page when you are
done with the last chapter!

Chapter 1
Start Your Engines

Hello! This is your **ROADMAPS** workbook. You are reading this workbook because somebody wants to help you learn to control your body, your thinking, and your feelings so that you will not get into trouble as you get older.

When you do all your work in **ROADMAPS**, your hard work will pay off and you will feel better about yourself. You will be a better problem-solver. People who care about you will be proud of all the good stuff you have learned and done. **ROADMAPS** is for boys and girls between the ages of 6 and 12, and for some older kids and grownups who get mixed up with big words.

Learning to change your behavior can be hard work. This work book will be your 4-wheel drive Jeep to help you get over even the worst road. By using this workbook, you will be on the right road to a healthy life!

Many boys and girls are now getting help for their touching problems. The good news is that by learning the skills in **ROADMAPS**, you will be able to prepare yourself for a happy and successful life.

ROADMAPS is hard work! With help from your counselor, parent, or foster parent, try to do a little bit every day. It might take a long time to finish **ROADMAPS**, but that is okay! It takes time to learn new behaviors.

Good luck with your travels in **ROADMAPS!**

By completing this workbook and sharing your work with your counselor, you will be able to join the sexual abuse prevention and safety team! Lots of other young people around the world who are living healthy lives have joined the team.

You will learn to be proud of your new behavior and accomplishments. Your counselor, parent, or foster parent may also set up rewards for you as you finish assignments and chapters. In **ROADMAPS** you will give yourself a sticker at the end of every chapter. The sticker means that you have worked hard and have earned an award for trying hard to be part of the sexual abuse prevention and safety team.

Now, here is your first assignment! This is so your counselor can get to know you a little bit, and you will even get to know yourself better. **ROADMAPS** can help in all parts of your life, so it is important to learn about who you are and how you think. It is okay to go ahead and write in this book.

Assignment #1A:

What is your full name? _____

_____

What is your birthdate? _____

What grade are you in? _____

What school do you go to? _____

_____

Where do you live right now? _____

_____

Who do you live with? _____

_____

What do you like to eat the most? _____

_____

What do you like to do in your free time?

_____

_____

What do you want to do when you grow up?

_____

_____

Do you have any brothers or sisters?

☐ Yes   ☐No

If you checked yes, write down the names
and ages of your brothers and sisters:

Name   Age

_____   _____

_____   _____

_____   _____

_____   _____

What are your hobbies? Do you collect stuff (like rocks or feathers or dolls or soldiers or beanie babies or trains)? _____

_____

_____

Do you have any pets right now?

☐ Yes   ☐ No

If yes, what type of pets do you have (dog, cat, snake, gerbil, goldfish, or ???) and what are their names?

Type   Name of Pet

_____   _____

_____   _____

_____   _____

Who is your best friend right now?

_____

_____

Who do you tell your secrets to?

_____

_____

Who in the whole world do you respect (look up to) the most right now? Who do you want to be just like when you grow up?

_____

_____

_____

You are doing great.
You are on the right road for safety!

Assignment #1B:
On the next 2 pages draw a picture of you, your pets, and your family. Then add other drawings or words about your favorite foods, things you like to do in your free time, and so on. In the drawing try to put in as much stuff from your first assignment as you can. You may use pictures or words. Have fun!

Good job! You have finished the first chapter! You are starting on the road to being a part of the sexual abuse prevention and safety team.

"Remember me? My name is Buzzbee. Follow me and I will show you the way to healthy touching."

Chapter 2
What Is A Touching Problem?

Warning: Read This Now! Some kids have very strong feelings when they work on their touching problems in **ROADMAPS**. Some kids get mad, or sad, and some kids get very strong sexual feelings in their minds and in their private parts. These feelings are normal.

Buzzbee says: "This could be a bumpy road, so fasten your seatbelts and get a good person to help steer you through!"

As you work through **ROADMAPS**, you might get new or strong feelings. Some kids want to hit something or do some sexual behavior. Having those kinds of feelings is normal, but doing the behavior could get you into trouble. Here are some ideas to help you stay out of trouble.

1. Tell your counselor about your feelings *before* you do anything with them.

2. Do something to move your body. Do sit-ups, play basketball, run around the block or your yard or a parking lot. Doing something physical helps make angry or sexual feelings go away.

3. Stop your work in **ROADMAPS** for a little while and tell an adult about your feelings. An adult will help you get back on the right road and back into **ROADMAPS** when you are ready.

Assignment #2A: Make a list of all the adults in your life you can tell when you are feeling angry or sad, or having sexual feelings:

1. _____

2. _____

3. _____

4. _____

5. _____

6. _____

ROADMAPS helps boys and girls who have touching problems. Anybody can have a touching problem, even teenagers and adults. Touching problems are easier to fix when you're younger.

A touching problem is when one person touches another person without permission, especially when the person's private parts are touched. Private parts are a person's bottom, chest, penis, and vagina. If you are not sure what those words mean, ask your counselor.

Touching problems are sometimes called sexual behavior problems.

When people get older, they sometimes touch each other's private parts. This kind of touching is called sexual touching, or just sex.

Sexual touching is not bad. In fact, one kind of sexual touching is how babies are made. Sexual touching can be fun and exciting when you're old enough. This kind of good sexual touching only happens when the two people both give their permission.

So, sexual touching can be a very good thing. It is not a good thing, however, when young children do it, or when it hurts or bothers other people.

Touching problems can also include things like touching your own private parts in public places, spying on other people when they are undressing, or talking too much about body parts.

Another kind of touching problem is when boys and girls touch animals in their private parts, or hurt animals with their touching.

One type of touching problem is called *incest*. Incest is when people in the same family who aren't already married touch each other's private parts. Incest is against the law. One reason is that if babies were made, they might have physical or mental problems. Another reason is that it hurts younger people when older people do sexual touching with them before they're old enough to understand. That is why people should not do sexual touching with other people in the same family.

There are many kinds of touching problems. In **ROADMAPS** you will get lots of help in stopping your wrong touching.

Your private parts are also called *sexual* parts. Sexual parts are parts of the body that have to do with sex. Sex is not bad, but some sexual touching is wrong touching, because it can hurt the other person or get you into trouble.

Some kinds of sexual touching are against the law, and sometimes people who do wrong sexual touching can go to jail. Children don't go to adult jail, but children who keep doing wrong sexual touching can go to special jails for children where they have to stay while they get help.

ROADMAPS will help you learn to control your touching so that you will not grow up and get in trouble.

There is one other problem that is kind of like a touching problem. It is called *sexual harassment.* This is when a person says or does something sexual that bothers another person and won't stop it. Here are some examples of sexual harassment:

1. Calling someone a sexual name.

2. Asking someone to do sexual touching when they have said no before.

3. Telling a sexual joke that bothers other people.

4. Showing sexual pictures to someone who doesn't want to see them.

5. Talking about a person's sexual body parts.

For example, one boy got into trouble at school for talking about the size of a girl's breasts on the school bus. The bus driver heard the boy and reported him to the principal. The hurtful way the boy was talking was sexual harassment.

Sexual harassment is not a good thing. People do sexual harassment to make someone else feel bad. Boys and girls can get into big trouble for it. You could get kicked out of school. When you get older you could lose a job if you do those behaviors at work.

Assignment #2B: Write down one other example of sexual harassment:

_____

_____

_____

_____

_____

_____

Here's what Ted had to say about his touching problem:

Hi, my name is Ted. I had a touching problem. My parents took me to a counselor because I was touching other kids in their private parts. I was about 7 years old when I was doing the private touching. Now I am 10 years old and I haven't done any wrong private part touching for 3 years. You should NOT be afraid in group. We try and help each other in group. I just told the truth to the other kids and my counselor.

Ted talked about having a counselor and being in a group. Counselors know how to help kids and grownups in lots of different ways. Your counselor can teach you how to control your body, your feelings and your thinking so you will not grow up and do wrong touching.

Groups are when three or more people sit down together with a counselor to talk about their problems. Groups help boys and girls with touching problems feel like they are not alone. Groups help boys and girls learn to control their bodies in good ways. Groups help boys and girls stay out of jail.

It is sometimes scary to be in a group to talk about private problems. Most boys and girls learn to like groups, because in groups they get support and help. Plus, it feels good to know that you are not alone.

Groups work best when everyone agrees to follow directions and rules. If you are in a group, your counselor may have all the boys and girls in the group make a list of their rules. Rules make group  a good, safe place to be. Here are some rules that you can learn to help your group be a safe place:

1. Arrive on time, leave on time. Show that you care by being ready on time.

2. Sit still in your chair. Sitting in groups is hard, but you can show you care about others if you stay in your chair.

3. Let one person talk at a time, and look at the person who is talking.

4. Show that you care about other group members. Listen to them, and do not talk when they are talking.

5. Ask questions about what the other group members said. This shows that you care.

6. When you hear a group member using right thinking, tell them they're doing a good thing. When you hear wrong thinking, try to nicely suggest something that would be right thinking.

When you follow these rules, your group will be a great place, and it will help you stay out of trouble!

Now it is time to get to know you a little bit more! **ROADMAPS** lets you share about yourself by drawing pictures. Have fun!

Assignment #2C: In this box draw a picture of yourself right now. Don't worry about how good your drawing is.

Assignment #2D: Draw a picture of someone you care about. You can draw more than one person. Ask your counselor to help you label each person in the picture. If you want, you can draw on a different piece of paper, and cut out the picture and paste it or staple it on this page.

Your picture can help you remember that you can care about people and they care about you.

You're doing great, traveling right along to the end of Chapter 2! You're following **ROADMAPS** to a better life and good adventures! Get a sticker for this page!

Buzzbee says: "Follow me! We're on the RIGHT road!"

Chapter 3
Right Touching
and Wrong Touching

Now it is time to learn about *right touching* and *wrong touching*.

Right Touching

Right touching is when you ask before you touch and the other person says it's okay. Right touching is when you touch someone in a nice and caring way.

Right touching is *legal*. You do not get in trouble for it. When something is *legal*, it is okay to do, and you will not go to jail if you do it. When something is *illegal*, it is not okay. You might hurt someone. You might get in big trouble if you get caught doing it.

Wrong Touching

Wrong touching is when you touch a person in a mean or hurtful way. Wrong touching is when you touch somebody else in their private parts without permission, even when you don't feel mean or you just want to share. Wrong touching is when somebody else touches you in your private parts without your permission.

Wrong touching is when you touch a person's private parts, and the person is more than 2 years younger than you. Or if the other person is not as smart as you. Or if you have to promise to give them some money or a present to get them to do it.

It's wrong touching if you make the other person feel scared that you will hurt them if they don't do what you want. Wrong touching is *illegal*, and you can go to kid's JAIL!

Wrong touching is when you touch private parts with somebody in your family.

Think about how it feels inside when you want to do wrong touching. Maybe you feel like wrong touching because you have done it before. If you have done it before, then it might pop into your mind when you are doing something else. Other children might not have the idea pop up in their minds because they didn't learn about wrong touching when they were younger. Other children might not be thinking about it, and they might not want to do wrong touching.

Remember, when you have sexual feelings, it doesn't mean that other people are having them too. They are your feelings. Your sexual feelings are not bad or wrong, but acting them out can get you in trouble and hurt other people.

Sometimes wrong touching feels very good for a little while. Wrong touching can make the person doing it feel strong, powerful, or excited.

Sometimes people don't understand why they should try to stop doing wrong touching. Here are some reasons that other young boys and girls came up with:

Why Should I Stop Wrong Touching?

1. I might get in trouble with my teacher.

2. Other kids will pick on me.

3. Other kids will tease me.

4. Other kids will hate me.

5. Other kids won't play with me.

6. I will get in trouble with my parents.

7. I might get in trouble with my treatment group.

8. I might get arrested by the police.

9. I might go to jail.

10. It might hurt the other person.

Now you have learned about what bad things might happen if you don't stop doing wrong touching. Here are some good things that might happen if you do stop doing wrong touching:

Good Things That Might Happen When I Stop Doing Wrong Touching

1. People will like me better.

2. It feels good to treat other people nicely.

3. My counselor will think I'm doing good in counseling, and will give me more play time.

4. My parents will be proud of me.

5. My teachers will be proud of me.

6. I will not go to kid's JAIL.

7. People won't think I am weird or strange.

8. I won't be afraid of getting into trouble as much.

9. I won't have to go to court and talk to a judge.

10. I won't grow up to be a sex offender!

Buzzbee says:
"I'm outa here.
No sex offenders for me!
I'm headed towards a healthy life."

Assignment #3A: Now it is your turn to talk about your own reasons for stopping your wrong touching. In the space below list some of your reasons for stopping your wrong touching:

1. _____

   _____

2. _____

   _____

3. _____

   _____

4. _____

   _____

5. _____

   _____

ROADMAPS will help you learn to stop behavior that hurts other people. Keep up the good work!

Now, let's see how this works in real life.

This next part of **ROADMAPS** is to help you decide what is right touching and what is wrong touching.

Assignment #3B: For each sentence, decide whether it is Right Touching or Wrong Touching. Circle the best answer and tell your counselor why you chose it.

1. My dad gives me a hug when I see him.

Right Touching   or   Wrong Touching

2. I run up to people when I see them and surprise them by jumping on them.

Right Touching   or   Wrong Touching

3. I touch my sister's private parts with my private part.

Right Touching   or   Wrong Touching

4. I shake hands with my counselor when I see him.

Right Touching   or   Wrong Touching

5. I hit people to see how they will react to me.

Right Touching   or   Wrong Touching

6. My mom rubs my back when I am tired.

Right Touching   or   Wrong Touching

7. My older sister had me put my penis in her private part.

Right Touching   or   Wrong Touching

8. Sometimes I touch my private parts when I am around other people.

Right Touching   or   Wrong Touching

9. A grown-up put his mouth on my private part.

Right Touching   or   Wrong Touching

10. Sometimes I kiss my boyfriend or girlfriend after asking if it is okay.

Right Touching   or   Wrong Touching

11. Sometimes I rub my private parts in front of my brother.

Right Touching   or   Wrong Touching

12. Sometimes I rub my private parts against someone when I am wrestling or playing.

Right Touching   or   Wrong Touching

13. My babysitter asks me to touch her private parts.

Right Touching   or   Wrong Touching

Great job! Take a break for a minute. Your counselor might have other examples like these that you can practice thinking about.

By learning the difference between right touching and wrong touching, you will have a much happier life!

Assignment #3C: Almost everybody does some right touching and some wrong touching as they grow up. Write down 5 examples of RIGHT touching that you have done in your life:

1. _____

_____

2. _____

_____

3. _____

_____

4. _____

_____

5. _____

_____

Great job!

Assignment #3D: Now write down 5 examples of wrong touching that you have done in your life:

1._____

_____

2._____

_____

3._____

_____

4._____

_____

5._____

_____

By writing these down and telling the truth you are using *Right Thinking*!

Good work! You are now done with Chapter 3. Get a sticker to put on this page! This was a hard chapter, and you did a good job.

Buzzbee says, "I'm proud of you!"

ROADMAPS TO RECOVERY

Chapter 4
Right Thinking
and Wrong Thinking

Nobody is *born* with a touching problem. Most boys and girls with touching problems start their lives in a normal way just like other boys and girls. Boys and girls with touching problems usually *learned* about wrong touching when they saw other people do it, or when someone else did it to them.

Later on in **ROADMAPS** you will have a chance to share more about where you learned your touching problem. Right now, it is time to learn about RIGHT THINKING and WRONG THINKING.

Do you know why you are learning about RIGHT THINKING and WRONG THINKING? It is because you are a human being! Human beings use their brains and their thoughts to control their bodies.

Yes, you might have guessed it, RIGHT THINKING leads to RIGHT TOUCHING, and WRONG THINKING leads to WRONG TOUCHING. If you can learn now about RIGHT THINKING, you will  have a much easier time staying out of trouble in the future.

There is another word for wrong thinking. Wrong thinking is also called "thinking errors." A thinking error is like a thinking mistake. So, wrong thinking is like making a mistake in your head. Wrong thinking is like taking the wrong road somewhere and getting lost or stuck in a dead end.

Leonard is 16 years old. He has learned about wrong thinking, or thinking errors. Leonard says:

"If you are 16 years old, and you are thinking about having sex with a 10 year old, that's a thinking error. That is wrong thinking, even if you didn't do it yet."

"If you think that people are always picking on you, that's wrong thinking."

"If you get in trouble for something, and decide to lie about it so you don't get caught, then that's wrong thinking. It is best to be honest and admit to what you have done."

"If you blame your behavior on other people, that is wrong thinking."

Tucker is 7 years old and is trying to learn to control his body and behavior. Tucker explains what he is learning about right thinking. Tucker says:

"Right thinking is when you tell the truth. Right thinking is when you admit to something you did wrong. Right thinking is when you think about other people, not just yourself."

"Wrong thinking is when you tell a lie. Wrong thinking is when you only think about yourself. Wrong thinking is when you blame other people."

Keenan, who is **9** and is getting help for his touching problems, has something to share, too.

"I was 8 when I did it. I feel guilty for what I did. I did some wrong touching with my younger sisters, who were 6 and 7. I felt sad when I got caught. I guess I didn't want to get caught. Now I am glad that I am getting help so that I will not have to go to jail."

Here are some more examples of RIGHT THINKING:

1. Thinking of how you can help other people, instead of acting selfish.

2. Thinking of being a good friend.

3. Deciding to let someone else go first at something.

4. Deciding to share something (but NOT your private parts!) rather than keep it to yourself.

5. Telling the whole truth about something you did.

6. Talking about what makes you worry.

Assignment #4A: One of the best ways to learn to stay out of trouble is to always use RIGHT THINKING. Give four examples of when you used RIGHT THINKING during the past week or two. You can ask your counselor or parents for help with this.

1._____

_____

2._____

_____

3._____

_____

4._____

_____

Assignment #4B: Now for a test! Read each sentence below and decide if it is right thinking or wrong thinking. Circle your answer. Your counselor will help you if you miss any.

1. Ricky tells his foster mother, "You are right, I did make a mess in my room."

Right Thinking   or   Wrong Thinking

2. Mary tells her mother that she did touch her little sister in her private parts.

Right Thinking   or   Wrong Thinking

This one could be hard to decide because Mary did wrong *touching*. Is telling the truth about it *right thinking* or *wrong thinking*?

3. Jeanne tells her friend that it is okay if she wants to play with her toys, and that she will play with her Nintendo.

Right Thinking   or   Wrong Thinking

4. John tells his father, "It is all your fault that I didn't do my chores."

Right Thinking   or   Wrong Thinking

5. Leroy always feels like people are mean to him, so he thinks it is okay to call them names to get back at them.

Right Thinking   or   Wrong Thinking

6. Mrs. King, the teacher, blames Bruce for losing a book, then she finds the book in her car.

Right Thinking   or   Wrong Thinking

7. 10-year-old Shawn has touching problems and doesn't have many friends his age. He thinks that he might as well play with the little kids, the five-year-olds, since they like him.

Right Thinking   or   Wrong Thinking

Great job! If there were some you didn't understand, ask your counselor or group for help.

Now you can learn another new word. The word is DENIAL. When you lie or don't tell the whole truth about something, that's DENIAL. Denial can also mean pretending something is not happening. Denial is like a roadblock in your way to getting where you are going.

Denial is one type of *wrong thinking*.

Here's Amber, who is 11, talking about why she denied at the beginning of treatment.

"I felt shy because I don't like talking about things that happened in the past. I especially don't like talking about sexual things because they make me feel squirmy inside. I have learned that I was in denial. Now I talk about my sexual behaviors because I have learned that it is okay to talk about them."

Lots of people use *denial* to cover up their mistakes so they will not get in trouble. Some adults use denial, too. A lie is a type of denial. When you lie you are denying the truth.

Look at the cartoon below. The man in the cartoon says he won fair and square, but the truth is that he used the wrong kind of force to get the other player to give up. This is one kind of denial.

To get very far in **ROADMAPS** it is important for you to *stop denying* and tell the whole truth. When you do, you will have a good life, and learn from the mistakes you have made.

Here is an assignment to help you stop using *denial*. You may want to ask your parent, your foster parent, or a group home staff member to help you with this assignment.

Assignment #4C: List three mistakes that you have told the truth about in the last month. For example, "I did take the quarter from the table;" "I did break the lamp;" "I did kick the dog;" "I did not turn in my homework."

1. _____

_____

_____

2. _____

_____

_____

3. _____

_____

_____

Now list three things that you lied about in the last month. It doesn't matter if you got caught in the lie or not. You may write any kind of lie you've told. For example, "I said I fed the dog when I didn't;" "I said I took a shower when I didn't;" "I said I didn't have any homework when I did;" "I said I ate all my vegetables when I gave them to my rabbit."

1. _____

_____

_____

2. _____

_____

_____

3. _____

_____

_____

Wow, you are really moving along fast now. Keep up the good work and you will be a great member of the sexual abuse prevention and safety team!

In **ROADMAPS** it is important to tell the whole truth. The faster you can overcome your denial, the more successful you will be.

"Wow, you are really moving! Denial is not for me. It's just a roadblock in my way!"

ROADMAPS TO RECOVERY ROADMAPS TO RECOVERY

Chapter 5
How To Stay Out of Jail:
Learning to Control My Body

Almost everywhere, children with sexual touching problems are given help so that they can learn to stop wrong sexual touching. If they are not able to stop by about age 12, they might get into serious trouble and they might have to go to jail.

Sandy is 11 and has been in counseling for about six months because of her touching problems. Here's what she has to say:

I have sexual problems, and I have touched other young kids in wrong ways. Sometimes it is hard for me to stop. I had a lot of sexual problems, and I almost got put in jail for them. I know one thing for sure — I do not want to go to kid's jail. If you are reading this book, then you probably have the same problem I do. So, if you have sexual problems, you better learn to control it, or you might end up hearing a judge tell you you're going to jail.

On the next page there are some rules about touching for you to learn.

Rules for Staying out of Kid's Jail:

1. Never touch someone's private parts if they are more than two years younger than you are, even if they say it's okay.

2. Never touch anybody in any way without getting permission first.

3. Do not touch your own private parts except when you are alone in a private place like your bedroom or the bathroom.

4. Don't even talk to younger children about sex or personal body parts.

5. Don't ever do anything that hurts another person.

Assignment #5A: In the space below, write ten good reasons to stay out of kid's jail. Think about it this way: why do you want to stay out of kid's jail?

1. _____

2. _____

3. _____

4. _____

5. _____

6. _____

7. _____

8. _____

9. _____

10. _____

In most places, even young children can be arrested by the police. In some places 8-year-olds can be arrested. In most places, sexual touching is against the law when one person is younger than 18 and the person doing the touching is more than 2 years older than the other person.

Some sexual touching can be okay, but only when both people want to do the touching, and when they are about the same age. If you are more than 2 years older than someone you want to do sexual touching with, and the other person is not 18, watch out because it might be against the law. Your counselor can teach you about the exact laws where you live.

It is probably against the law if the other person is younger, or doesn't understand about sexual touching, or doesn't give permission and you touch the person's private parts anyway.

It is against the law if you get permission to do sexual touching by giving the person presents or money. Or if you say you'll hurt the other person or break the person's toys or hurt the person's pets or a family member or a friend. Those are quick ways to end up in kids' jail for wrong touching.

Remember these rules:

1. Only do sexual touching with persons who are the same age as you (never more than 2 years younger).

2. Never use force, threats, or presents and bribes to get someone to do touching with you.

3. Don't do sexual touching with family members. Sexual touching with family members is against the law (illegal).

Here are some examples for you to think about. Decide if they are legal or not legal. Remember if they are not legal, the person can be arrested by the police.

Assignment #5B: Circle the right answer for each situation.

1. Mary is 9. Beth is her best friend's 5-year-old sister. Mary kisses Beth and touches her private parts while playing hide and seek.

Legal   Not Legal (illegal)

2. John is 10. One day he and his 10-year-old friend, Josh, show each other their penises.

Legal   Not Legal (illegal)

3. Jasmine is **8**. One day she tries to get her 4-year-old brother to touch her private parts.

Legal	Not Legal (illegal)

4. Miguel is **11**. While babysitting his 8-year-old cousin, he puts his penis in his cousin's bottom.

Legal	Not Legal (illegal)

5. Jeremiah sometimes gets very mad. One day while at school he grabs the private parts of another boy, hurting the other boy.

Legal	Not Legal (illegal)

Your counselor will help you figure out if your answers were right or wrong. Don't worry if you missed some of the right answers. The point is to learn about this stuff now so you don't grow up with wrong ideas that get you in trouble!

In **ROADMAPS** you are learning that your brain controls your body, just like the driver controls the car.

You are learning to always use *right thinking*. Some kids with touching problems have other problems that are important to work on also, like Michael.

Michael is in counseling for a touching problem with his sisters. One day at school he gets into an argument with Jordan. Michael calls Jordan a name, then he hits Jordan. Jordan gets mad, and tries to choke Michael. Michael then grabs some scissors and chases Jordan. When the teachers break up the fight they suspend Michael from school for chasing Jordan with scissors.

Michael was mad at first that the teachers suspended him and not Jordan, because he thought he was right, and Jordan started the argument. When he talked with his counselor, he realized that he was using wrong thinking, and that he wasn't controlling his body in a good way. His brain was working in the same mixed-up way it was when he abused his sisters.

Assignment #5C: Write down 5 times you did not control your body as well as you should have during the past two weeks: (Examples: Not doing a chore, calling someone a name, hitting something, breaking something, acting lazy, etc.)

1. _____

_____

2. _____

_____

3. _____

_____

4. _____

_____

5. _____

_____

Assignment #5D: Now write down 5 times that you controlled your body in a good way during the past two weeks: (Examples: doing a chore, doing homework, talking about mad feelings, calming myself down, being careful with toys, ignoring people who pick on me, etc.)

1. _____

   _____

2. _____

   _____

3. _____

   _____

4. _____

   _____

5. _____

   _____

In **ROADMAPS**, it is important to work on controlling your body in good ways all the time. Not just with your sexual touching, but everyday, in all parts of your life. Remember, you are learning to change your behavior and the way your brain works. You are learning about Right Thinking! **ROADMAPS** is like driver education, learning how to control your body like a driver controls a car. Doing it the right way keeps you safe. Doing it the wrong way puts you and others in danger.

Great job! You can put your sticker on this page. You can also decorate this page with drawings. Keep up the good work. Follow Buzzbee to learn more about staying out of trouble.

"Follow me! Using Right Thinking means we're on the right track!"

Chapter 6
Building Up My Walls to Stop Wrong Touching

In this chapter you will learn about the walls that usually keep people from doing wrong touching. You will learn how your walls got broken down, and how you can build them up again to stop wrong touching.

There are four walls that keep people from doing wrong touching:

1. Normal Relationships

2. Inside Walls

3. Outside Walls

4. Victim's Resistance (Doesn't Want To)

Let's look at each one.

1. Normal Relationships

Everybody gets urges to do sexual touching at some time in life, just like everybody gets urges to buy things. People get the urge to do wrong sexual touching when they do not have normal, healthy relationships.

Normal healthy relationships are ways that you get along with others so that you feel loved and smart and good, without hurting each other. In normal, healthy relationships, we also feel loving and caring. We give as well as getting.

When we feel loved and smart and good, our needs are being met. There are 3 kinds of needs that we all have; Body Needs, Brain Needs, and Love and Attention Needs. In a Normal Healthy Relationship, those needs are met.

BLOCKAGE is when things happen that keep you from getting what you need. When you are blocked from getting your needs met, it is hard to have a normal healthy relationship. You may find yourself trying to get your needs met in unhealthy ways. That is when you might feel an urge to do wrong sexual touching and hurt someone.

BODY NEEDS: These are the things that you need from other people — your family and friends, that have to do with your body. Things like food, water, clothes, a safe and warm place to sleep, and someone to

help you take care of yourself. Some other body needs include exercise, space to move around, light and fresh air. These things help you feel strong and healthy and good.

BRAIN NEEDS: These are the things that have to do with liking yourself. They are things that your mind needs so you can believe that you are smart enough, good enough and able to do  stuff. Things like compliments, good grades, rewards, manners, things you like to do that you are good at help you meet your brain needs.

LOVE AND ATTENTION NEEDS: These are things that help you feel loved and needed and wanted. They are about feelings. Love and Attention needs are things like people listening to you while you speak, getting hugs, having friends, feeling safe, people trusting you, being able to say and hear things like, "I love you."

Let's look at how this works:

Davey Ant is a bank robber. His parents have both died, and he has no other family. Davey was fired from his job, and now he doesn't have enough money to buy gas or pay his rent. He feels lonely and bad inside, and he doesn't think he is good enough or smart enough to get another job. Davey is blocked, and tries to get his needs met by robbing banks, even though it hurts people.

Assignment #6A: Write down what you think Davey's body needs are.

_____

_____

_____

What is blocking Davey from getting his body needs met? Write it here.

_____

_____

_____

What are his brain needs? Write them here.

_____

_____

_____

What is blocking Davey from getting his brain needs met? Write it here.

_____

_____

_____

What are Davey's love and attention needs? Write them here.

_____

_____

_____

What is blocking him from getting his love and attention needs met?

_____

_____

_____

Now let's talk about you. You might have also been blocked. You might have tried to get your needs met in a way that hurt other people. You didn't rob any banks, but you might have hurt someone. Or you might have done wrong sexual behavior.

Buzzbee's friend, Rita, is here to help you with this work. Rita's answers to the questions on the next few pages may give you some ideas about your needs and how they were blocked. Rita is 10 and lives in a foster home. She was sexually abused by her older brother and her

parents. That means that her older brother and her parents did wrong sexual touching with her. She also did wrong sexual touching with some younger boys in another foster home.

Assignment #6B: Read each question. Then read Rita's answers to help you. Then write your own answers. Your answers may be different from Rita's answers.

What kinds of body needs did you have before you did wrong sexual touching?

Rita: "Having a stable place to live, and having enough food to eat. I also needed some space of my own and some privacy."

_____

_____

_____

_____

What blocked you from getting your body needs met?

Rita: "I was sexually abused. My parents didn't watch me or take care of me. We didn't have a place to live. Sometimes we slept in the car."

_____

_____

_____

What kinds of brain needs did you have before you did wrong sexual touching?

Rita: I really needed to be able to think I was smart and that people loved me.

_____

_____

_____

What blocked you from getting your brain needs met?

Rita's answer: I was sexually abused, and my family always moved around. I was always changing schools, and I never felt like I fit in.

_____

_____

_____

What kinds of love and attention needs did you have?

Rita: Feeling safe and having a warm place to sleep. I wanted to have people spend time with me.

_____

_____

_____

What blocked you from getting your love and attention needs met?

Rita: I lived in a homeless shelter, and my parents used drugs, and never had time for me.

_____

_____

_____

Great job! Now let's look at the Inside Wall.

2. Inside Wall

Everybody has two walls — an INSIDE WALL and an OUTSIDE WALL.

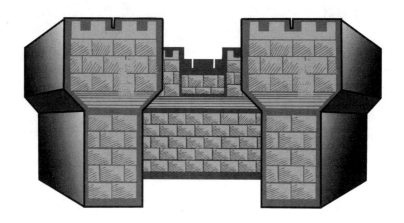

These walls help keep us from making bad choices and doing things that hurt ourselves or other people.

Your INSIDE WALL is that little voice inside of you that tries to stop you from doing something wrong. "Don't do it," says the voice. "Someone will see, you'll get in trouble!! It's bad! It's wrong!! It'll hurt the other person! You wouldn't like it if somebody did it to you!" All of the thoughts and feelings that should stop you before you hurt somebody are the bricks that make your Inside Wall.

Don't do it, it's wrong!

Davey, the bank robber, had an Inside Wall, too. His little voice told him that robbing banks was wrong. He knew that it was against the law. He felt scared of getting caught, and guilty because the money was not his.

Assignment #6C: What did the bricks of your Inside Wall look like before you did wrong sexual touching? Think of as many of the thoughts and feelings you had that should have made you stop before you did wrong sexual touching to someone else. (Rita will help you by sharing her answers. Think of your own answers after you read hers, and write them down.)

Rita: They might tell. This is bad. I might get in trouble.

1. _____

_____

2. _____

_____

3. _____

_____

These inside walls usually do their job. They stay high enough or long enough or thick enough to stop us from making wrong choices. But sometimes we hurt others or do wrong things anyway. We do this by using WRONG THINKING.

WRONG THINKING IS ALSO CALLED MAKING A THINKING ERROR. You learned about the difference between Right Thinking and Wrong Thinking in Chapter 4.

THINKING ERRORS are lies that we tell ourselves so that we ignore the things that our little voice is trying to tell us. We are using Thinking Errors when we pretend for awhile that our little voice isn't telling us the truth. We build a *ladder of lies* so we can crawl over our Inside Wall and make that bad decision anyway.

Davey used Thinking Errors to keep lying and tricking himself until his ladder was tall enough to climb over the top of his Inside wall.

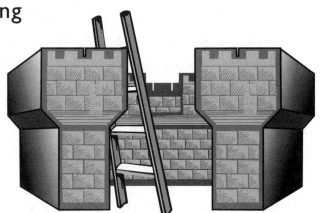

His little voice said "it's wrong."

Davey said "I don't care."

He knew it was against the law.

Davey said "I'll only do it once."

He was scared of getting caught.

Davey said "I won't get in trouble."

He felt bad about stealing.

Davey said "I deserve it — I need it."

Assignment #6D: Think about some of your wrong touching. What kinds of lies did you build your ladder with?

Rita: It won't hurt anybody.
He won't tell.
I'll just do it a little.

1. _____

_____

2. _____

_____

3. _____

_____

Now let's look at the third wall, the Outside Wall.

3. Outside Wall

Your OUTSIDE WALL is made up of the things outside of your body that should have stopped you before you did wrong sexual touching.

The Outside Wall is a lot like the Inside Wall, but you have to work harder to get over it or through it. Each brick in your outside wall is something that made it hard for you to be alone with the person you touched sexually.

PLANNING is what you did to try and get through your outside wall. Your wall was full of bricks that should have stopped you. You had to do a lot of planning to be able to touch the person that you touched.

Those plans were like cannon balls and blasting powder that you put in a cannon so you could blast your way through your Outside Wall.

Davey, the bank robber, had an Outside Wall. Davey's wall was made up of all the people who were at the bank, the big, thick door on the vault, and the guard and video cameras that were watching the bank. These were things that were outside of himself that should have made it really hard for him to rob that bank.

Assignment #6E: List some of the things that made it easier for you to do wrong touching. These are the things that made weak places in your Outside Wall.

Rita: I wasn't being watched.
I watched the sexy movies.
I slept in the same room with the little boys.

1. _____

_____

2. _____

_____

3. _____

_____

Davey loaded his cannon with plans like waiting until the people left, making sure that he had the combination to the safe and spraying paint on the cameras so they couldn't see him.

Assignment #6F:
What plans did you load your cannon with?

Rita: I waited until grownups were gone. I shut the door to the room, so the other kids couldn't see.

1. _____

   _____

2. _____

   _____

3. _____

   _____

Your Outside Wall is important, and if you work to build your wall as big as you can, it will help you not do wrong touching again. In the next chapter you will make a list of rules that will keep your outside wall very strong. When your wall gets big enough and thick enough, the cannons won't be able to break through it. Making sure you are not alone with younger kids will help.

The last wall to learn about is the VICTIM'S RESISTANCE (Doesn't Want To) wall.

4. VICTIM'S RESISTANCE

(Doesn't Want To)

First you were BLOCKED and chose to find other ways to meet your needs. Second you built a ladder of THINKING ERRORS to ignore your little voice and climb over your INSIDE WALL. Third, you filled a cannon full of PLANS and blasted your way through your OUTSIDE WALL.

The last thing you had to do before you did wrong touching was to get past the victim's resistance. Resistance is when a person fights against something the person doesn't want to do.

Your VICTIM'S RESISTANCE was the way that the person you did sexual touching with tried to stop you. You were probably older, bigger, smarter, stronger or the boss of the people that you touched.

Assignment #6G:
What were the things that the victims — the kids you did wrong sexual touching with — did or said to try and stop you?

Rita: They said go away, leave me alone.
They tried to get out of the room.

1. _____

   _____

2. _____

   _____

3. _____

   _____

There are 4 ways that people get around the victim's resistance: PROMISES, PRESENTS, THREATS and FORCE.

These are ways of getting people to do what you want them to do, even when they don't really want to.

PROMISES are things that you did or said that the victim might have liked.

"If you do this then I will _____."

The promises that fill in the blank can be things like being the person's friend, letting the person ride your bike, taking him or her to play video games or go rollerblading.

Assignment #6H:
What kind of things did you promise the kids you touched?

Rita: I said that I wouldn't tell the grownups. I said I would be their friend if they let me touch them.

1. _____

_____

2. _____

_____

3. _____

_____

PRESENTS are things you give the person so he or she will let you do wrong touching. Maybe you gave the victim some money, or one of your favorite things, or you took the victim to get ice cream or pizza after you did the touching. Sometimes these kinds of presents (where you get something back) are called bribes.

Assignment #6I: What kind of presents did you give (or promise to give) the kids so they would let you touch them?

Rita: I gave one my allowance. I gave another one my dessert for a week so he would let me touch him.

1. _____

_____

2. _____

_____

3. _____

_____

THREATS are things you did or said that the victim didn't like. "If you don't do this then I will_____." In this blank go things like not being the victim's friend or telling the victim you would hurt him or her, or break the person's favorite toy, or hurt the person's dog, or tell the victim's parents.

Assignment #6J:
What kind of things did you threaten your victims with?

Rita: I said if they told I would say it was their fault. I said I would not be their friend any more unless they let me touch them.

1. _____

   _____

2. _____

   _____

3. _____

   _____

FORCE is when you grabbed the victims or held them or hurt them to make them do what you wanted.

Assignment #6K:

What kind of things did you do to force the victims to do what you wanted?

Rita: I ignored them when they said no, and I touched them anyway in their private spots. I took one boy's hand and put it on my private area.

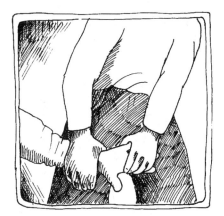

1. _____

   _____

2. _____

   _____

3. _____

   _____

As you work through **ROADMAPS** you will learn how to build up all of your four walls so that you can become a member of the sexual abuse prevention and safety team. These walls are like safety rails on a twisty highway. They keep you from going off track and hurting yourself or other people.

You are learning to control your *Urges*, use *Right Thinking*, follow good *Safety Rules*, and respect other people. By doing this, you will learn to enjoy normal healthy relationships.

Great work. This was a hard chapter, and it is very important.

Buzzbee says:
"I am proud of you.
Keep following me!"

Chapter 7
Making and Following
My Safety Rules
(Keeping My Walls Strong)

Some young people with touching problems live with younger children. When you live with younger children, it is very important to follow special rules. Rules help people stop wrong touching. Rules are like bricks that  build up your Inside and Outside walls. Rules help young people stay away from kid's jail!

Josie, age 7, has touching problems. She made some rules for herself with her counselor's help. Josie had touched both of her younger brothers in their private parts before she started treatment. These rules help her not do wrong touching. They help Josie's younger brothers feel safe.

Josie's Rules
for Staying out of Trouble

Here are some rules that Josie made up to help her stop doing sexual touching.

1. Don't sneak up on brothers.
2. Don't be alone with them at all, unless an adult is around and watching.
3. No punching, touching, or grabbing.
4. Do not wrestle with my brothers.
5. Do not go into brothers' bedrooms for any reason.
6. Do not play house with brothers.
7. Do not talk about sex with brothers.
8. No going in bathroom when anyone is in there.

I agree to always follow these rules:

Josie L.   January 14, 1999

Buzzbee says:
"Rules help keep us safe.
Rules are good bricks in our
inside and outside walls.

Assignment #7A: Now make up your own list of rules that will help you avoid wrong touching:

1. _____

_____

2. _____

_____

3. _____

_____

4. _____

_____

5. _____

_____

6. _____

_____

7. _____

_____

8. _____

_____

Bryan is 11. When he was 9, he did sexual touching with a 6-year-old girl. Bryan has been in counseling for 2 years to work on his sexual behavior. When Bryan started counseling, he did things like cover his face when he talked. He also would do rude things like flip his legs up so that his bottom was showing. Bryan didn't know how to talk to people or be with them in a nice way.

Bryan has learned some treatment rules that have helped him get along better in his foster home and at school.

I have to always ask before touching a person. Before I started counseling, I would just walk up to a person and put my arms around them. Sometimes I would sit or stand so that I was touching the other person. Now I know about personal space. We also call it boundaries. A boundary is like a personal bubble around a person. Now I have a 3-foot rule. With my rule I try to stay 3 feet away from other people unless I have permission to get closer.

With these rules, Bryan has been able to stay out of jail, and he is feeling very happy that he has been getting along better with other kids.

Boundaries are like fences around things that you want to keep private, just for yourself. Boundaries protect things you own, like your CD player. Boundaries can be around things like your room, your clothes, or your treatment notebook.

You can also have boundaries around your feelings or past experiences. Sometimes people don't like to talk about their father, mother, or their childhood because they feel bad. They have a boundary around talking about their families.

Boundaries help people live together in families or neighborhoods. Boundaries say, "This is mine, please respect that." That is why your friend can't just walk off with your toys or music, and it is why people who steal go to jail. It is important to have boundaries so we can feel safe with others.

We all have a right to tell other people what our boundaries are, especially when they have to do with keeping our bodies safe. Here are some of Bettina's boundaries:

1. I don't like people touching my face.

2. I don't like people using my clothes.

3. I don't like people talking to me about my mother.

4. I don't like people getting too close to me, it makes me nervous.

Assignment #7B: In the space below write down some of your personal boundaries. Be creative, and you can list any boundaries you can think of:

1. _____

_____

2. _____

_____

3. _____

_____

4. _____

_____

5. _____

_____

Assignment #7C: Now ask your counselor what the boundaries are in his or her office. Find out what things you can touch, and what things you should leave alone. Write down the things you should leave alone in the space below:

1. _____

2. _____

3. _____

4. _____

5. _____

6. _____

Assignment #7D: This assignment is for you to do at home. Sometime during the next week ask your parents, foster parents, or group home staff what their boundaries are in their home. Ask them what their physical boundaries are. You might have to tell them what a boundary is. Write down what they say in the space below.

What is the name of the person you talked with?

_____

What are their physical boundaries at home?

1. _____

2. _____

3. _____

4. _____

5. _____

Remember, healthy people respect other people's boundaries! Respecting boundaries means staying away from whatever is inside the boundary. By respecting people's boundaries, you will stay out of kid's jail. You will also have more friends when you respect boundaries!

Buzzbee says,
"Leave my engine alone,
that's my boundary!"

ROADMAPS TO RECOVERY

Chapter 8
Talking About Touching That People Have Done To Me

In **ROADMAPS** you are learning to control your wrong sexual touching. One way to do this is to learn where you learned about wrong sexual touching. Once you figure out where you learned about wrong sexual touching, it will be much easier to STOP!

Because you are young, learning to STOP doing something can be easier than it is for adults. You are always learning, and it is never too late to learn new things.

Assignment #8A: Your life! Draw a picture of your *past* life, how it used to be. You can include your house, your family, or anything else. Your counselor will help you label everything in the picture. You can pick any time in your past life you want.

Assignment #8B: Think about where you first learned about sexual touching. Remember what you saw in person, on T.V., or what happened to you. Think about your past. Now answer these questions (if you don't think anybody ever touched you, just put "none" in the blanks):

1. Who was the first person who ever touched you in a sexual way?

_____

2. How old were you when it happened?

_____ years old

3. How old was the other person?

_____ years old

4. What did that person do?

_____

_____

_____

5. Where were you living when it happened?

_____

_____

6. How did you feel when the other person did the sexual touching to you?

_____

_____

_____

_____

_____

_____

7. Who was the second person who ever touched you in a sexual way?

_____

8. How old were you when it happened?

_____ years old

9. How old was the other person?

_____ years old

10. What did that person do?

_ _

_ _

11. Where were you living when it happened?

_ _

_ _

_ _

12. How did you feel when the other person did the sexual touching to you?

_____

_____

_____

_____

_____

13. Now list any other people who have ever touched you in your private parts, or had you touch them in their private parts.

_____

_____

_____

_____

Assignment #8C: What is the earliest thing you can remember about your life? Think about when you were very young. Write down what you remember:

_____

_____

_____

_____

_____

_____

It will help you stop your wrong sexual touching if you start talking about your feelings instead of keeping them inside.

Talking about your feelings with a good friend or an adult who cares about you is a very healthy thing. Learning to talk about feelings is an important part of Roadmaps. You may want to talk about feelings you had when someone did wrong sexual touching to you. Or you may want to talk about other feelings you have every day.

Here are some people you might want to try talking to about feelings:

> your mom or dad

> your counselor

> your foster parents

> the grownups at the group home

> a school counselor or a teacher you like

> an aunt or uncle or grandparents

> your best friend

There are some people you might NOT want to talk to about your feelings:

> people who did wrong touching to you

> people who tell other people what you tell them without your permission

> people who make fun of you for talking about feelings

Assignment #8D: Make a list of people you know you can talk to about your feelings.

1. _____

2. _____

3. _____

4. _____

If you were touched by an older person, you might have some feelings inside that you don't tell other people about. Boys and girls who have been sexually touched by older people have lots of different feelings. Here is a list of some:

Scared	Bored/empty
Confused	Ashamed
Angry	Guilty
Sexy	Hurt
Lonely	Helpless

Sometimes it also helps to draw a picture about what happened to you. Sometimes pictures work better than words.

Assignment #8E: In this space, draw a picture about another person touching you in a way you didn't like. Ask your counselor to help label each person in the picture. If you want, you can draw on a different piece of paper, and cut out the picture and paste it or staple it on this page.

What would you say if you could tell the person who touched you how you felt about it? What would you want that person to say or do? Even when the other person is not in your life any more, it is still a good idea to try to tell the person about your feelings about the touching. You can do this in a letter. Maybe you will want to send the letter, but maybe you won't. For now, try to get your feelings down on paper, and your counselor can help you decide later what you should do with the letter.

Here's what you could put in the letter:

1. Start with a greeting, like "Hello, Billy."

2. Write how old you are now, and where you are living (not your address, but something like, "I live with my Aunt Jane now" or "I live in a group home now.")

3. Say what you remember about the kind of touching the person did to you.

4. Say how you felt when it was happening.

5. Tell the other person what you want him or her to do (for example, "I want you to stop touching kids and get help" or "I don't want you to write to me").

6. Sign the letter with your name.

Here is a letter Marcus wrote to his older half-sister, who had done sexual touching with him.

July 1, 1999

Dear Beth,

I am 9 years old right now, and I am living in the Smith foster home. I can't live with Aunt Debbie any more because I did wrong touching with Sara and Lisa. I remember that I learned about touching from you when I was 4 years old. You were about 6 or 7 years old. I can remember that we were at dad's old house in the city. I can remember that we were in the blueberry patch together, then in the bedroom together. I remember that I had to go to the bathroom. You told me that I could put my peepee in your peepee. I think you wanted to keep my peepee in your peepee longer than I did. I remember that it happened two times in one day.

I really don't know how I felt about it back then. Right now I don't feel very good about what you did to me.

I want you to stop touching kids. I think you should go to a counselor too to get help. I also want to know why you touched me in the private parts.

Thank you for listening to my feelings. I do care about you since you are my sister.

Your brother,
Marcus

Now it is your turn to write a letter to a person who touched you or hurt you. Your counselor can help you decide who you should write the letter to. Remember, the main purpose of the letter is to help you get your feelings out.

Your counselor will also help you decide if you should send the letter or not. If you are in a treatment group, it is a good idea to share the letter with other group members. If it is the right thing for everyone, your counselor may even help you meet with the person who touched you so that you can talk about the letter in person.

Assignment #8F: Follow the steps you read a couple of pages ago, and write a letter to the person who touched you or hurt you.

Date:_____

Dear _____,

_____

_____

_____

_____

_____

_____

_____

_____

_____

_____

_____

Assignment #8G: Now share your letter with someone you trust. If you are in a treatment group for people with touching problems, you may also share it with them. Ask a person you shared the letter with to write down what they liked about it in the space below.

Person's Name: _____

What the person liked about the letter:

_____

_____

_____

_____

Buzzbee knows that you are doing hard work, and he has some advice. "Remembering things from your past can bring up bad feelings. Sharing those feelings can also help you feel better. Keep on truckin, you're on the right road!"

ROADMAPS TO RECOVERY ROADMAPS TO RECOVERY

Chapter 9
Telling The Truth About My Wrong Touching Behavior

In this chapter you will be asked to share about your own touching problems. This might be hard. Talking about wrong touching can be scary, embarrassing, or just plain hard. But you *can* do it, and it will help you get on the right road and stay out of kids' jail.

Remember back in Chapter 4 when you learned about denial? Many people have problems with denial. In **ROADMAPS**, you don't have to worry about people judging you, or getting into trouble. In **ROADMAPS** we know that it takes a strong and brave person to talk about wrong touching problems.

Some people have a hard time admitting mistakes they make. It's hard to tell the truth about something you did that hurt someone else or when you broke a rule. Sometimes people even lie and make up stories to keep from getting caught and getting in trouble. In **ROADMAPS** it is important to keep on doing *Right Thinking* and not do *Wrong Thinking*. It's like following a good paved road and not taking any turns onto bumpy dirt roads that lead to dead ends. Admitting your past mistakes is keeping on the right road. By doing this, you get rid of your denial, and you will be making real progress!

Telling the truth about what you did is like taking your car to the mechanic. The mechanic can't fix what's wrong if you make up a different story and don't tell what's really happening. If the car is backfiring, but you say the brakes are squealing, the backfiring problem probably isn't going to get fixed.

In **ROADMAPS** you have to admit (tell the truth about) your past wrong touching so that you can make a good safety plan to keep from doing it again in the future. Your counselor, parent, or foster parent will help you use the information to make a good plan.

Assignment #9A: You probably have some reasons and some feelings about why you don't want to tell the truth about your wrong touching. Write down three of them:

1. _____

_____

2. _____

_____

3. _____

_____

Assignment #9B:

Now write down five reasons for telling the whole truth about your touching problem:

1. _____

_____

2. _____

_____

3. _____

_____

4. _____

_____

5. _____

Next you will make a list of every person you touched in a sexual way. This helps you get rid of secrets. Keeping secrets about sexual touching is not good. Keeping secrets about wrong touching doesn't help you stop. Keeping these secrets is like a false road sign that will send you right to kids' jail! It's time to take the lid off your can of secrets.

Assignment #9C: In the spaces on the next pages, write the name of a person you touched, then answer the questions. If there are more spaces than victims, just write *No More* in the extra spaces.

1. Person's name: _____

Person's age when you touched: _____

Your age when you touched: _____

Which private parts did you touch? Circle what you touched:

penis   vagina   bottom   breasts   mouth

What did you touch the person with? Circle what you used to touch:

penis   hand   finger   mouth   breasts   object

How many times have you done sexual touching to this person? _____

Where were you living when you did the touching to this person? _____

_____

2. Person's name: _____

Person's age when you touched: _____

Your age when you touched: _____

Which private parts did you touch? Circle what you touched: _____

penis   vagina   bottom   breasts   mouth

What did you touch the person with?
Circle what you used to touch:

penis   hand   finger   mouth   breasts   object

How many times have you done sexual touching to this person? _____

Where were you living when you did the touching to this person? _____

_____

3. Person's name: _____

Person's age when you touched: _____

Your age when you touched: _____

Which private parts did you touch? Circle what you touched:_____

penis   vagina   bottom   breasts   mouth

What did you touch the person with? Circle what you used to touch:

penis   hand   finger   mouth   breasts   object

How many times have you done sexual touching to this person? _____

Where were you living when you did the touching to this person? _____

_____

4. Person's name: _____

Person's age when you touched: _____

Your age when you touched: _____

Which private parts did you touch? Circle
what you touched:_____

penis   vagina   bottom   breasts   mouth

What did you touch the person with?
Circle what you used to touch:

penis   hand   finger   mouth   breasts   object

How many times have you done sexual
touching to this person? _____

Where were you living when you did the
touching to this person? _____

_____

5. Person's name: _____

Person's age when you touched: _____

Your age when you touched: _____

Which private parts did you touch? Circle
what you touched: _____

penis   vagina   bottom   breasts   mouth

What did you touch the person with?
Circle what you used to touch:

penis   hand   finger   mouth   breasts   object

How many times have you done sexual
touching to this person? _____

Where were you living when you did the
touching to this person? _____

_____

6. Person's name: _____

Person's age when you touched: _____

Your age when you touched: _____

Which private parts did you touch? Circle what you touched:_____

penis   vagina   bottom   breasts   mouth

What did you touch the person with?
Circle what you used to touch:

penis   hand   finger   mouth   breasts   object

How many times have you done sexual touching to this person? _____

Where were you living when you did the touching to this person? _____

_____

Good job! Admitting and telling the whole truth about your own sexual touching problems is a very big step in your treatment. If you have been honest with this assignment, then you can be very proud of yourself.

Buzzbee says,
"You are doing a great job.
Keep on moving!"

Chapter 10
Understanding How I Have Hurt People & Apologizing For My Wrong Touching

Now it is time to think about how your actions have hurt other people. You can't change your past behavior, but you can join the Sexual Abuse Prevention and Safety Team by apologizing for your past mistakes. Apologizing helps you feel better about your past mistakes, and it helps other people feel better about you too!

Here is what Kaitlyn, age 9, wrote to her 6-year-old brother Karl. She wrote the letter after she had been in counseling for about four months.

January 23

Dear Karl,

I am very sorry I hurt you in the private parts. I am getting help now. I will not do it again! I can remember touching and hurting you on the privates about 10 times with my hand. I also touched you and made you put your penis in my private parts 4 times. I can understand why you are sometimes scared to be around me. What I did to you was very wrong. I am working in counseling so I will not hurt you again.

I will not chase you at school, because I don't want you to feel scared. I am also going to follow all of my treatment rules from now on.

Your sister,

Kaitlyn

Your letter should cover these points:

1. Today's date.

2. A greeting (like "Dear" or "Hello") using the person's right name.

3. An apology (saying "I'm sorry") for your wrong touching.

4. Write exactly what you did to the other person. Write how you touched him or her. Say how many times you did it.

5. If you lied about it or blamed it on the other person, admit it.

6. Write that the touching was your fault and not the victim's fault.

7. Say what you are doing to stop your wrong touching.

8. Give another apology for your wrong touching.

9. Promise to not hurt or touch the other person again (but only if you really mean it and want to keep your promise).

10. Sign your name!

Assignment #10A: Look at the list of things that should be in the letter. Read Kaitlyn's letter again. Write the number of each thing from the list next to where it is in Kaitlyn's letter. For example, put a number 1 next to the date on Kaitlyn's letter.

Are all the things on the list in Kaitlyn's letter? Did Kaitlyn leave anything out?

Write down the numbers of the things on the list that you did not find in Kaitlyn's letter: _____

_____

Assignment #10B: Now it is your turn to try writing a letter to the person you touched in a wrong way. Maybe you can do a better job than Kaitlyn did. Remember to write only things that are true and that you really mean.

Start your first letter on this page. You can number each part of the letter if it helps you remember what to write. Don't worry if you mess up! Your counselor can give you more paper to write another copy of the letter.

Date: _____

Dear _____,

_____

_____

_____

_____

_____

_____

_____

_____

_____

_____

_____

_____

_____

_____

_____

_____

Sincerely,

_____

Great job. This is a very hard part of treatment. You might get to send the letter if your counselor thinks it would be a good idea. You might even get to meet with the victim and some counselors so you can apologize. Apologizing in person takes someone who is brave and strong, and usually everybody feels better afterwards.

Now you can draw a picture in the space below, or ask your counselor for a sticker. Don't forget to keep track of your progress on the chart at the beginning of **ROADMAPS**.

Buzzbee says: "You are on my team, the sexual abuse prevention and safety team!"

Chapter 11
Learning to Talk About
My Feelings

In this chapter you will learn how to talk about what is going on in your body and in your thoughts in a healthy way. You will learn about feelings. Everybody has feelings every day. Some people are better at talking about feelings. Some boys and girls only know how to talk about happy or angry feelings. Other boys and girls know about lots of different feelings. In **ROADMAPS** it is very important that you learn to talk about lots of different feelings, not just happy or angry feelings.

By learning to talk about feelings, you learn to get what you want without hurting other people. Let's learn three new words:

The first word is *passive*. Passive means quiet, calm, or not doing anything. Passive people don't react very much. Passive people stay very calm, and nothing bothers them. Passive people don't yell or fight. Sometimes they let people make decisions for them, even when it's not what they want. Sometimes people who are passive are angry and don't know it or show it. Shy people are often passive.

The second word is *assertive*. Assertive people say what they think and ask for what they want. They are not passive, they do speak up for themselves, and they hardly ever let other people make decisions for them. Assertive people express their feelings without hurting or scaring other people.

The third word is *aggressive*. Aggressive people are pushy and sometimes demanding. They don't think about how their behavior affects other people. Aggressive people sometimes scare other people, because they are loud and sometimes mean. Bullies are often aggressive.

Assignment #11A: Learning to be assertive: read the sentence, then decide if the behavior is passive, assertive, or aggressive. Circle the correct answer.

1. Suzy is mad at her foster mom. She wants to call her friend on the phone, but her mom won't let her. She tells her mother that she is upset, and she tells her mother she wants to talk about it.

Passive   Assertive   Aggressive

2. Josh is unhappy about his birthday party plans. He decides to sit in his room and listen to his music.

Passive   Assertive   Aggressive

3. Cory wants to play Nintendo, but his parents have put the controllers away. He yells, "You are never fair." He then slams the door and kicks a chair, breaking it.

Passive   Assertive   Aggressive

Assignment #11B: Practicing being assertive:

1. Read about Betty's problem below and write an assertive response for Betty to use.

Betty is mad because the staff members at her group home want her to help with the dinner dishes.

Assertive Response: _____

_____

_____

_____

_____

2. During the next week try to be assertive at least three different times. Keep track of when you act assertive by telling how you feel, and asking for what you want.

A. _____

_____

_____

_____

B. _____

_____

_____

_____

C. _____

_____

_____

_____

These three words, *passive*, *assertive*, and *aggressive*, describe different ways of expressing feelings. Passive people don't express their feelings enough, while aggressive people express their feelings in a mean or hurtful way. *Assertive* people express their feelings clearly, without hurting or scaring other people. In **ROADMAPS**, we hope that you will learn to be *assertive*.

To learn more about how you can be *assertive*, first we'll learn about what makes you happy and angry.

Assignment #11C: List four things that make you feel happy:

1. _____

2. _____

3. _____

4. _____

Assignment #11D: Now list four things that make you angry:

1. _____

2. _____

3. _____

4. _____

Assignment #11E: List four other feelings you sometimes have inside of you (such as sad, lonely, scared, sexy, frustrated, curious, loving, hungry, tired, cold and so on):

1. _____

2. _____

3. _____

4. _____

Anger can be an excuse for not feeling other feelings. In **ROADMAPS**, we want you to think about how you use anger as an excuse not to share other feelings.

Anger is a normal feeling that most people get some times. People who get angry *all* the time can be described as *aggressive*. It is not good to be angry *all* the time. In fact it's no fun at all. People who are very angry usually are not very good at talking about their other feelings. So, think of anger as just an excuse for not telling what you are really feeling.

Will is 10 and lives in a group home. Will used to get mad a lot, and staff often had to hold him down to keep him from hurting people or breaking things. As Will went through counseling, he learned that he has lots of other feelings. He is unhappy that his parents abused him, and he feels strange and sad that he doesn't have a regular home to live in. He is also feels bad about himself for sexually touching his sister. Will also is very lonely, and he doesn't feel like other kids want him for their friend.

A funny thing has happened. As Will has learned to talk about his life, he has learned about lots of different feelings. Before he started talking about his feelings, all he knew was anger. So Will has learned that his anger was just an excuse for the other feelings he was having. Now Will can be *assertive*, and speak up without hurting other people. He feels a lot better and is starting to make friends.

Assignment #11F: In the space below, write down as many feeling words as you can. It is okay to ask for help from your counselor or parents.

1. _____

2. _____

3. _____

4. _____

5. _____

6. _____

7. _____

8. _____

9. _____

Assignment #11G: Now let's play a matching game. Draw a line from each feeling word to the situation that matches the word.

Lonely	Playing with someone I like
Happy	Bedtime
Frustrated	Getting up too early in the morning
Hungry	Not having many friends
Tired	Doing fun things
Grouchy	Getting a hug before I go to bed
Sad	Going to the waterpark
Unloved	Having a family
Excited	Getting into trouble
Friendly	Seeing the bad guys win on T.V.
Loving	Lunchtime
Joyful	My pet died

Assignment #11H: Think about the last two weeks. Using your own experiences, finish these sentences:

1. I felt excited when: _____

_____

2. I felt frustrated when: _____

_____

3. I felt loved when: _____

_____

4. I felt happy when: _____

_____

5. I felt sad when: _____

_____

6. I felt confused when: _____

_____

7. I felt lonely when: _____

_____

LEARNING TO TALK ABOUT MY FEELINGS

8. I felt proud when: _____

_____

9. I felt afraid when: _____

_____

10. I felt unhappy when: _____

_____

You are doing great. Keep it up!

Now you can mark your progress chart, or collect a sticker from your counselor. Keep it up and you will be good at telling about your feelings.

Buzzbee says, "I'm feeling breezy and relaxed. I'm really moving along now!"

Chapter 12
Understanding My Cycles

In this chapter you will learn another way to make good changes in your life. Did you ever know somebody who always seems to have problems and keeps doing wrong or bad things over and over again? Somebody who always seems to be in trouble? It is like this person just can't seem to do right things for very long. He or she just keeps getting into trouble. This person is in a cycle.

Cycles are things that repeat over and over again. Night→day→night→day — that is a cycle. Up→down→up→down — that is another cycle.

Another cycle you might see in your life is: Hungry→eat→play→hungry→eat→play→hungry. Cycles can be healthy (good) or unhealthy (bad).

Cycles go around and around, around and around, just like car wheels and bike wheels. Sometimes they go so fast that it's hard to see the spokes that make up parts of the cycle.

Listen again to Ted, age 10, who has been in counseling for a long time.

Sometimes I kept doing wrong things. It was like a weather cycle to me. In a weather cycle, it gets cloudy, it starts to rain, then the rain dries up and evaporates back up into the sky. Then the cycle starts all over again.

Ted has learned that everybody has cycles of behavior, just like a weather cycle. He has learned that by getting ready for it, he can control himself better.

In order to change your bad cycles of behavior, you have to learn to pay attention to the *early warning signs* of your cycle. In a weather cycle like the one that Ted described, the *early warning sign* is the cloudy weather.

Like Ted said, if you learn to watch the sky, you have a better idea of when you might need an umbrella — or when to put the top up on a convertible.

ROADMAPS is going to help you understand your cycles. Think about times when you did wrong touching. What was happening in your life just before you did the wrong touching? Usually, it was something that made you feel mad or sad or upset or weak. Thinking about the wrong touching and planning how to do it made you sort of feel better for a while.

Here are some things that Rita, Ted, Amber and Bryan wrote about what was happening just before they did wrong touching:

1. I was touched in my private parts by another person.

2. I was moved into a foster home.

3. I was watching sexy movies with pictures of naked bodies.

4. My brother touched my private parts.

5. I was always getting into trouble.

Assignment #12A: Now make your own list of things that were happening in your life before you did wrong touching:

1. _____

2. _____

3. _____

4. _____

5._____

6._____

7._____

8._____

In Chapter 15 you will make some plans that will help you make good choices whenever you are having bad experiences in your life. By making good choices, you can stay out of *negative* cycles.

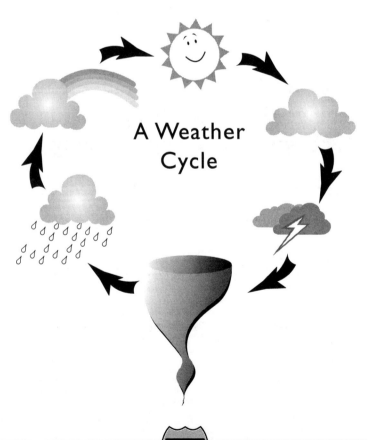

A Weather Cycle

Here is an example of a behavior cycle: Justin was usually a happy person. Sometimes he got mad, though, and when he got mad, he broke things and yelled at people. After he broke things, he often felt bad. Here is how his cycle looked when it was put into a chart:

Justin's Behavior Cycle

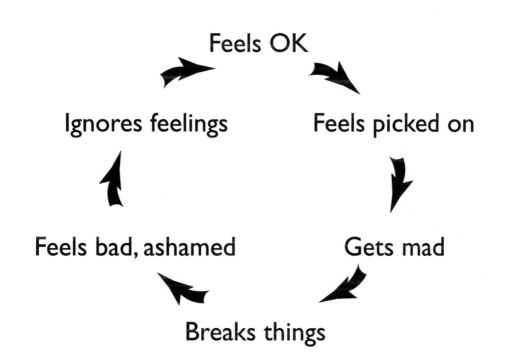

With the weather cycle, the best way to cope with the rain and the storms was to watch for the clouds. In Justin's case, the best way to control his yelling and breaking behavior is to pay attention to when he feels mad or picked on. When he feels that way, he can then do healthy things to get his feelings out. For him, that is like putting up the umbrella.

If you were in a car or on a bicycle and you came to a fork in the road, how would you decide which way was the right way? Having a map would help. That is a good way to prevent being lost. **ROADMAPS** shows you how to take the right turns so that you can develop healthy behavior cycles. Looking at your cycles is like drawing a roadmap.

In the next set of assignments you will be filling out a chart of your own cycle of wrong touching. It's like drawing a map of where you took wrong turns or ignored the clouds that were bringing a rainstorm of trouble.

Assignment #12B: Think about how you did your wrong touching. What feelings came before you did it? In the chart on the next page, write those feelings in the spaces marked "Feelings Before."

Feelings Before

_____

_____

_____

How
I felt
after

What
happened
next?

_____ Notice where _____

_____ you use your _____

_____ umbrellas _____

My wrong touching

_____

_____

_____

Assignment #12C: What happened next? How did you feel about it? Write that in the spaces marked "What happened next?"

Assignment #12D: What wrong touching did you do? How you did you feel while you did it? Write it in the spaces marked "My wrong touching."

Assignment #12E: What feelings did you have after you did the wrong touching? Write them in the spaces marked "How I felt after."

Good job! Now you are beginning to see some of the parts of your cycle about wrong touching.

Now that you've learned about your cycle of wrong touching, you can use cycles to look at other problems, like being angry (remember Justin's cycle?) Here are some problems that other kids have worked on with cycles:

1. Angie gets mad at staff where she lives and she often ends up yelling bad things.

2. Billy has problems getting along with other kids, and he starts a lot of fights by calling them names.

3. Suzanne steals things from other people at school.

Assignment #12F: What are some other problem behaviors you have? Do you get mad all the time? Do you not want to share the stuff you like to play with or read with anyone else? Do you throw your clothes and stuff on the floor? List three problem behaviors in the spaces below.

1. _____

2. _____

3. _____

Assignment #12G: Now pick one or two of these problem cycles to work on. Use the chart on the next page as your worksheet. Fill it in completely. There is an extra copy of the chart to use later in case you have other problems to work on.

After you fill out the chart, complete the assignments.

Feelings Before

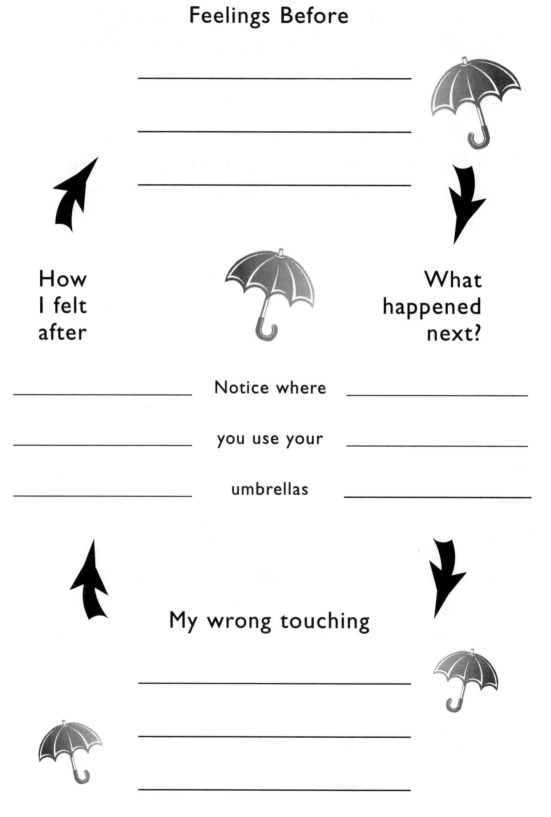

_____

_____

_____

How
I felt
after

What
happened
next?

_____   Notice where   _____

_____   you use your   _____

_____   umbrellas   _____

My wrong touching

_____

_____

_____

Feelings Before

_____

_____

_____

How I felt after

What happened next?

_____ Notice where _____

_____ you use your _____

_____ umbrellas _____

My wrong touching

_____

_____

_____

Assignment #12H: Putting up your umbrellas: In the space below, list as many positive and healthy things you can do when you notice your bad feelings that lead to you day-to-day behavior problems. These things are all your umbrellas.

1. _____

2. _____

3. _____

4. _____

5. _____

Buzzbee says, "Here comes a rain storm. I can see the clouds. I better turn on the windshield wipers."

ROADMAPS TO RECOVERY

Chapter 13
What Should I Do When I Get Those Sexual Feelings?

A lot of you who are reading **ROADMAPS** have something very important to look forward to. That important thing is called *puberty*. Most boys and girls start puberty anywhere from age ten to age twelve. If you are older, you may be going through puberty now. Or maybe you've already been through puberty. Reading this chapter will help you remember what that was like.

When puberty comes, your body changes in many ways. Hair grows under your arms, and on your private area. If you are a boy, your voice might also get deeper. If you are a girl, your breasts start to grow and you may begin your monthly cycle, called *menstruation* (say men-strew-AY-shun).

In puberty, your body is helping you get ready to be a young man or woman. In Chapter 14 you will learn a little bit more about the changes that come with puberty.

Another thing to look forward to is your sexual feelings. Everybody gets sexual feelings sometimes. Sometimes sexual feelings are called urges. Remember them? You learned about urges in Chapter 6.

Sexual urges happen to everyone. Some people use different words to describe this feeling. One way some people describe having sexual feelings is "feeling horny." In **ROADMAPS** you never have to be afraid or ashamed of your sexual feelings. It is okay to talk with your counselor, parent or foster parent about your sexual feelings. You can't get into trouble for having sexual feelings, but you can get into trouble for doing wrong touching.

Here are some ideas that Jacob, 9, came up with. He has been learning how to control his sexual feelings and urges:

I have learned that masturbation is okay. Masturbation for boys is when you rub your penis. I have learned that it can make you feel good without hurting other people. I have learned that it is best to masturbate in private when nobody else is watching you.

When I get urges to do sexual touching I tell myself to calm down. I also do fun things like sports to keep my mind off it. Sometimes when I am really worried about doing wrong touching I tell an adult. I also think about what might happen in the future if I do wrong touching. When I think about getting into trouble I stop my urges.

Here is a list of ten things you can do to help yourself control your sexual urges.

1. Go tell an adult.

2. Masturbate in private.

3. Play a game to get your mind off of it.

4. Tell your brain to stop, and think about what might happen in the future.

5. Get some serious physical exercise to wear yourself out.

6. Do 50 sit-ups in your bedroom.

7. Quickly get away from any younger children.

8. Think about how awful it would be to go to kid's jail.

9. Think about how other people would feel disappointed in you.

10. Yell *NO* inside your head, and do something else.

Assignment #13A: List all of the people that you feel safe enough with to talk to about your sexual feelings, masturbation, and urges:

1. _____

2. _____

3. _____

4. _____

5. _____

Assignment #13B: Now pick one of the people from your list. Talk to that person about your sexual feelings this week. You might want to ask the person what ideas he or she has about controlling sexual feelings.

Person's Name: _____

Have the other person write down what you said and then sign this paper.

What I said: _____

_____

_____

_____

_____

_____

Signature: _____

Assignment #13C: List three things that work for *you* to help control your sexual feelings:

1. _____

2. _____

3. _____

Remember, everybody gets sexual feelings as they grow older.

Sexual feelings are not bad, they are perfectly normal.

It is your job to learn how to control your sexual feelings so that you don't hurt other people, and so that you don't get into trouble.

Buzzbee says,
"Even I want to go
too fast sometimes.
I have to learn to use my
brakes."

Remember to mark your progress chart.
You may also draw a picture or put a
sticker on this page.

Chapter 14
Understanding My Changing Body

In the last chapter, you read about some changes in your body that happen as you grow older. As your body changes, you might find that you have more and more sexual thoughts and feelings. In this chapter, you will learn a little bit more about how your body works.

As boys and girls get to be between 11 and 13 years old, their bodies start to change. This change is called *puberty*. *Puberty* is the time when your body changes from being a child into being more like an adult. Some boys and girls start puberty earlier than age 11 and some start later than age 13. It's all a normal part of growing up.

During puberty your body grows very fast, and many changes happen. The main thing you will see is that body hair starts growing under your arms and around your private parts. Girls may notice that their breasts are starting to grow bigger. Other changes are going on inside you that you can't see. This is an exciting time!

During puberty, boys start making *sperm*, and a white liquid containing sperm comes out of their penises when they masturbate and have an orgasm or ejaculate (say "ee-JAC-yew-late).

Masturbation is when boys touch or rub their penises or girls touch their clitorises and it feels very good. A girl's clitoris is a little bump inside the outer lips of her private parts. It's very sensitive to touch and can make a girl feel all excited inside.

Sperm is the part of a boy or a man that swims up inside a girl or a woman and joins with an egg to make a baby.

When girls get to puberty, their bodies start making tiny eggs ready every month. Each egg could become a baby. Girls know they've started making eggs when they start having monthly *periods*, also called menstruation (say "men-strew-AY-shun"). All through the month, their bodies have been busy using blood and other matter to make a home for an egg to grow in. If the egg doesn't need its home that month, it drains out from a girl's vagina. That is menstruation or a monthly period.

An egg only needs the new home if a boy's sperm swims up inside and joins with the girl's egg. If that happens, the egg is *fertilized*. A fertilized egg attaches to the cushion of blood, and a baby starts growing.

Your counselor will help you understand the drawings of boys and girl's sexual parts.

Boy's Private Area And What's Inside:

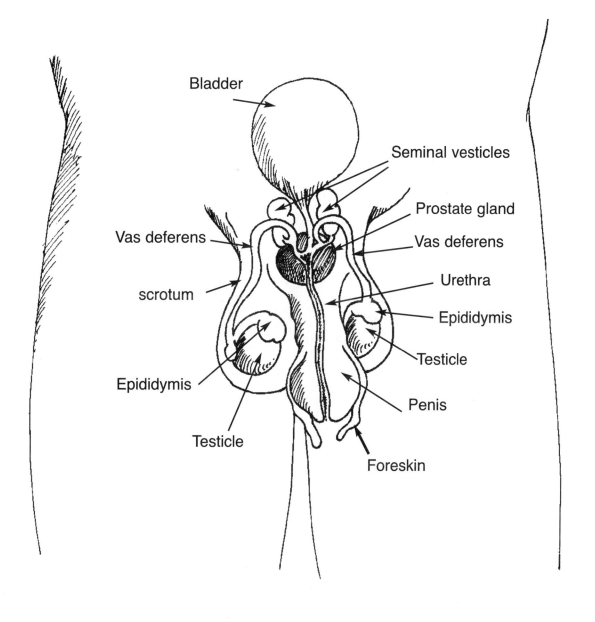

Bladder

Seminal vesticles

Prostate gland

Vas deferens

Vas deferens

Urethra

Epididymis

scrotum

Testicle

Epididymis

Penis

Testicle

Foreskin

Girl's Private Area And What's Inside:

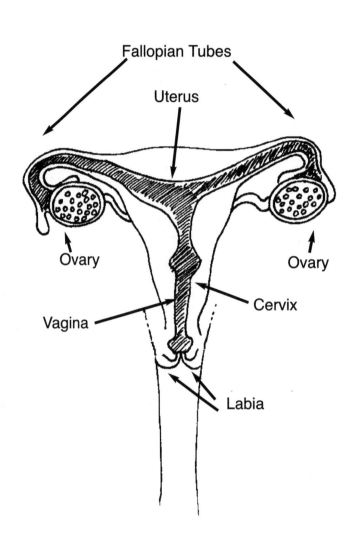

Bodies are very special and wonderful things, and if you make *good choices*, your body will bring you lots of fun and exciting times, including sex. By understanding how your body works, you won't have to feel worried or ashamed about the things you feel in your body.

You can also see why our bodies are private. And why each person has a right to decide his or her own body boundaries.

It is also up to you to show that you are in charge of your own body. You can show this by being healthy and clean and taking good care of your body. Some of the ways healthy people take care of themselves are listed here. As you read the list, put a checkmark in the box next to the things you do to care for yourself.

❏ Bathe or shower every day.

❏ Brush teeth twice a day.

❏ Comb my hair.

❏ Wear clean clothes.

❏ Change my underwear every day.

❏ Trim and clean my nails when I need to.

❏ Wash my hands after going to the bathroom.

❏ Wash my ears with a washcloth.

Talk to your counselor and your group about how you take care of yourself. Gently remind others in group if they need to work harder on keeping clean and healthy.

Sometimes looking healthy also means respecting your body and other people in public by keeping yourself from doing things that might embarrass you, your family, or friends.

Here are some tips:

1. Blow your nose with tissue, don't pick it.

2. Try not to suck on your fingers, toes, pencils, erasers, and shirt sleeves (try a peppermint instead).

3. Keep your feet off the furniture.

4. Keep your hands in *right touching* places.

5. Zip up your pants zippers all the way all the time (except when you are using the bathroom).

6. Speak clearly, not too loud, not too soft.

7. Quietly say "Excuse me" when you pass gas. Try to move away from other people when you do it.

PASS WITH CARE

8. Don't joke about other people's bodies. Everyone wants to like their own body. Respect that!

9. Be friendly, but respect other people's boundaries. If you want to have friends, be friendly, not pushy.

Buzzbee says,
"I like friendly people."

Mark your progress on your progress chart and draw a picture or put a sticker on this page! Good work, you are doing GREAT!

ROADMAPS TO RECOVERY ROADMAPS

Chapter 15
Making My Safety Plan And Sharing it With Others

Now that you have made it this far in **ROADMAPS**, you are very close to becoming a full member of the sexual abuse prevention and safety team. But first you need to share what you have learned with other people, so that you will have a *support team* to help you later on.

Your support team is made up of the people you can talk to about your wrong touching problem. Some of the team members will be family members and other helping adults. Having a support team is like having a fire extinguisher in your house. It protects against problems!

In this chapter you make a safety and prevention plan and share it with other members of your support team. Your support team is like the pit crew for race car drivers. They help you fuel up, change the tires, and get you back in the race. They let you know how well you're doing and when it might be time to come in for refueling.

Your Prevention and Safety Plan is made up of different parts. Remember your basic rules for staying out of kid's jail? They are the first part of your Safety and Prevention Plan. Here's a reminder:

1. Never touch someone's private parts if they are more than two years younger than you are.

2. Never touch anybody in any way without asking for and getting permission first.

3. Do not touch your own private parts except when you are alone in a private place like your bedroom or the bathroom.

4. Don't even talk to younger children about sex or personal body parts.

5. Don't ever do anything that hurts another person.

These rules are very important. They should always be part of your safety plan. If you follow your safety plan, you won't drive off the safe road.

Building your safety plan:

Now you get to build on that first part, the rules for staying out of kids' jail, by putting together everything you have learned. Your job is to make a safety plan that you can share with your support team, the people who care about you. Your support team will help steer you right and get you back on the road in case you make any mistakes or take any wrong turns.

A safety plan is like a big, strong wall that keeps you safe from driving off a cliff. The wall keeps you away from trouble. Look at the wall on the next page, and think about how it can protect you from trouble.

Now imagine your wall crumbling. When you don't use your safety plan, your safety wall starts to crumble too.

If you ignore your safety plan for too long, the wall that was keeping you safe really starts to fall apart. When it falls apart, trouble can come right through the wall and find you. Or you can drive right through it and over the cliff.

Look at this picture. Once the safety wall has started to crumble, it can't protect you any more.

Assignment #15A: On the next page, draw a picture of "Trouble" coming through your own wall when it has broken down. What does "Trouble" look like for you? Are there any words that go with "Trouble"? Write them in.

To make your safety plan strong and to keep your wall strong, start by making a list of your *warning signs*. Warning signs are signals that you might be making a bad choice. One kind of warning sign is when you see a dark cloud, you know that it might rain.

Think about all the things that happened to you before you did your wrong touching. Think about the hurt, sad, bad, mad, scared, hard feelings you were feeling before you did wrong touching. The things that happened and the feelings you felt are all warning signs.

Assignment #15B: On the left side of the list below, write as many things as you can that might be warning signs for you. A warning sign is anything that might mean that you are getting closer to doing wrong touching. Every warning sign you write is like putting another brick in your safety wall.

My Safety Plan

Warning Sign	Positive Plan
1. _____ _____	1. _____ _____
2. _____ _____	2. _____ _____
3. _____ _____	3. _____ _____
4. _____ _____	4. _____ _____
5. _____ _____	5. _____ _____
6. _____ _____	6. _____ _____
7. _____ _____	7. _____ _____

What I Can Do to __ What I Don't Do That

Stay Safe   Gets Me in Trouble

_____   _____

_____   _____

_____   _____

_____   _____

_____   _____

_____   _____

I agree to help _____
follow this plan as much as I can.

Signed: *Date:*

_____   _____

_____   _____

_____   _____

Assignment #15C: On the right side of your list of warning signs, write some positive things that you can do to solve the problem without hurting anyone.

For example:

Warning Sign	Positive Plan
Fighting at school	Talk about my feelings.
	Walk away instead of fighting.
Sneaking & spying on people	Tell myself to STOP. Think about boundaries. Do something else, like watch a movie. Tell my counselor or my parent what I feel like doing.

Assignment #15D: On the second page of your Safety and Prevention Plan, make a list of things you could be doing to stay safe. Write the things that you like to do (like play checkers or computer games) and add the things that you have to do (like chores and homework).

Assignment #15E: On the other side of the page, write the things that might get you closer to wrong touching (like babysitting or playing with little kids at the park). This is your list of things NOT to do, because they might help you get in trouble.

Assignment #15F: Have as many people as possible who care about you sign your plan. When they sign your plan, they become members of your support team. The more people you have sign it, the better your support team will be.

Assignment #15G: Thick as a brick: Each space in this box is a brick in your wall. Fill in as many bricks as you can with ideas about how to avoid trouble. Each brick is part of your safety plan. If you can fill in every brick, you wall will be strong and Trouble cannot climb over or bash through. Ask your counselor for a highlighter to make the filled-in bricks shine.

Example: Play a lot of sports or walk or ride bikes

Example: Talk about my feelings

Remember to pay attention to your warning signs. Ignoring your warning signs is a lot like crossing the street without looking both ways.

Not noticing your warning signs is like not noticing the road sign that warns of a sharp curve in the road ahead. Watching for warning signs will keep you from driving off the road.

Keep your safety plan and check it now and then. Later on you may need to add things to your safety plan. Your warning signs or the ways you solve the problems might change. If you use your safety plan, you will be prepared for any trouble that might come up.

Assignment #15H: Making Your Safety Plan Book: Okay, you have traveled a long road to get this far. Buzzbee is very proud of you. Your support team is also proud of you. Now you have one final project to do before you can say that you have finished **ROADMAPS**. You will make a Safety Plan Book. A Safety Plan Book is a notebook or folder that you put together yourself. Your counselor will give you the basic supplies you need for your Safety Plan Book. For your book you will need these supplies:

1. Scissors

2. Paper and pens or markers for coloring

3. Construction paper or poster board

4. Clear tape

5. Colored paper and plain white paper

6. Paper punch

7. Yarn or very heavy string

Let's get started! This project might take a few weeks to finish. Your counselor might change your directions to make them work better for you. The first thing to do is to make a cover for your book.

Directions:

1. Find six large pieces of colored construction paper or poster board. They should be about 18 inches wide, and at least 24 inches long. Put the paper in a stack so that all the edges line up. This will be a big book!

2. Take the paper hole punch and punch three holes in the paper on the left side. Put one hole at the top, one in the middle, and one at the bottom, very close to the edge (about 1 inch from the edge).

3. Next take three pieces of yarn or heavy string and loop one piece through eachhole. Tie each piece together so it makes a loose loop. This is your binder that holds the book together.

4. Now you have have a big empty book with six pages, including the front and back. On the front, take your markers and design a cover. The cover should include the words "My Safety Plan Book." Put your name and the date on the cover. You can make the cover look however you want it to. You can draw pictures on it, make a colored border, or even put stickers on it. This is your book, so make it look as good as you can!

5. Now comes the important stuff. On the inside pages of your Safety Plan Book you should put the important things you have learned in **ROADMAPS**. Here are some ideas:

A. You might want to have your counselor make copies of important pages in **ROADMAPS**, then tape the pages in your book. For example, your safety plan book should include a copy of your safety plan on one of the pages.

B. You might also want to copy the list of people you can talk to about your sexual feelings.

C. The page listing ways to control your sexual urges is also a good page to put in the book. You can copy it yourself on plain paper with a colored marker, or you can have your counselor copy it for you.

D. Sometimes it is a good idea to put a copy of your cycle in the book from Chapter 12.

E. Making a list of things in your life that make you happy (from Chapter 11) is also a good idea.

F. This is your book, and you should put as much as you can into it. You can put in a list of right touching and wrong touching, and you can also put in some examples of right thinking and wrong thinking. You can keep this book to remind you of how to live a healthy life.

6. Now decorate your book so that you can be very proud of it. You can put a picture of yourself in the book. You can also put a picture of your family or your counselor in the book. This is your book, so make it just like you want it to be.

7. Check your book. Make sure it is full of good reminders. Ask for suggestions from your counselor about what else you might want to add (maybe your certificate from the end of this book).

8. **You are done!** Share your book with members of your safety plan team. You have done some hard work!

Great Job! You have finished **ROADMAPS**. You have done a lot of work. It is almost like finishing a cross-country trip or a long race.

You have come a very long way. You now know that you can think like a responsible person, and you know how to share your feelings with others in a good way. It is up to you to use your new skills every day. You can be proud of yourself, because you are now part of the **sexual abuse prevention and safety team**.

This Is To Certify That

_____

Is Hereby Awarded

Membership in the Sexual Abuse Prevention and Safety Team

for
Completing Roadmaps to Recovery

_____   _____
Counselor   *Date*

If you are a good reader, you may want to ask your counselor for other treatment workbooks. Since you have finished **ROADMAPS**, you now are ready to graduate to the next level. There is another workbook called *Pathways* that can teach you even more about how to stop your wrong touching problems.

For now, you should feel proud that you did all the work in **ROADMAPS**.

Congratulations!

A Note of Thanks

This book was written with the help of many young boys and girls who worked very hard to learn to control their sexual behavior problems. You know who you are, and I am very proud of you all. I would also like to thank the many staff in Cottage A (WINGS Program) and Cottage D at Ryther Child Center in Seattle for their dedication to working with boys and girls with sexual behavior problems, and their help in developing the Roadmaps workbook. I particularly would like to thank Roger Iino, Karen Brady, Robert Strauss, Kimberly Panos, Lisa Kiesel, and Adam Wallas for their support and ongoing comittment to helping children with sexual behavior problems.

Special thanks go to Sherri Ford, Greg Merrill, Carol Almero, Nick Wiltz, Mary Meinig, Charles Lund, Heather Chambers, and Greg Hunter, for their helpful comments and ideas regarding Roadmaps. Jo Langford also provided helpful ideas and text for Chapter 5, and his assistance was greatly appreciated.

My wife, DeeAnn, provided much helpful support and encouragement. Also, my three children, Krishan, Kory, and Kyle all provided inspiration and help with this project. Thank you!

Timothy J. Kahn
Bellevue, Washington

Buzzbee says, "You did it! You're a part of the sexual abuse prevention and safety team!"

Select Safer Society Publications

Pathways: A Guided Workbook for Youth Beginning Treatment by Timothy J. Kahn (3rd Edition 2001). $22.

Pathways Guide for Parents of Youth Beginning Treatment by Timothy J. Kahn (3rd Edition 2002). $10.

Del Camino (Spanish version Pathways, 3rd Edition 2001) by Timothy Kahn $24.

STOP! Just for Kids: For Kids with Sexual Touching Problems Adapted by Terri Allred and Gerald Burns from original writings of children in a treatment program (1997) $15.

The Relapse Prevention Workbook for Youth in Treatment by Charlene Steen (1993). $18.

Tell It Like It Is: A Resource for Youth in Treatment by Alice Tallmadge with Galyn Forster (1998). $15.

Feeling Good Again by Burt Wasserman (1999). A treatment workbook for boys and girls ages 6 and up who have been sexually abused. $16.

Feeling Good Again Guide for Parents & Therapists by Burt Wasserman. (1999). $8.

When Children Abuse: Group Treatment Strategies for Children with Impulse Control Problems by Carolyn Cunningham and Kee MacFarlane. (1996). $28.

From Trauma to Understanding: A Guide for Parents of Children with Sexual Behavior Problems by William D. Pithers, Alison S. Gray, Carolyn Cunningham, & Sandy Lane (1993). $5.

Shining Through: Pulling It Together After Sexual Abuse by Mindy Loiselle and Leslie Bailey Wright (1997). $16. For girls aged 10 and up. New material on body image, self-esteem, self-talk, and sexuality.

Back on Track: Boys Dealing with Sexual Abuse by Leslie Bailey Wright and Mindy Loiselle (1997). $14. A workbook for boys ages 10 and up. Foreword by David Calof.

Adolescent Sexual Offender Assessment Packet by Alison Stickrod Gray & Randy Wallace (1992). $8.

Female Adolescent Sexual Abusers: An Exploratory Study of Mother-Daughter Dynamics with Implications for Treatment by Marcia T. Turner & Tracey N. Turner (1994). $18.

Man-to-Man, When Your Partner Says NO: Pressured Sex & Date Rape by Scott A. Johnson (1992). $8.

The Secret: Art & Healing from Sexual Abuse by Francie Lyshak (1999). $22.

Outside Looking In: When Someone You Love Is in Therapy by Patrice Moulton and Lin Harper (1999). $20.

Web of Meaning: A Developmental-Contextual Approach in Sexual Abuse Treatment by Gail Ryan & Associates. (1999). $22.

Female Sexual Abusers: Three Views by Patricia Davin, Ph.D., Teresa Dunbar, Ph.D., & Julia Hislop, Ph.D. (1999). $22.

Cultural Diversity in Sexual Abuser Treatment: Issues and Approaches edited by Alvin Lewis, Ph.D. (1999). $22.

When You Don't Know Who to Call: A Consumer's Guide to Selecting Mental Health Care by Nancy Schaufele & Donna Kennedy (1998). $15.

Sexual Abuse in America: Epidemic of the 21st Century by Robert E. Freeman-Longo & Geral T. Blanchard (1998). $20.

Assessing Sexual Abuse: A Resource Guide for Practitioners edited by Robert Prentky and Stacey Bird Edmunds (1997). $25.

Impact: Working with Sexual Abusers edited by Stacey Bird Edmunds (1997). $20.

Supervision of the Sex Offender by Georgia Cumming and Maureen Buell (1997). $25.

A Primer on the Complexities of Traumatic Memories of Childhood Sexual Abuse: A Psychobiological Approach by Fay Honey Knopp & Anna Rose Benson (1997) $20.

The Last Secret: Daughters Sexually Abused by Mothers by Bobbie Rosencrans (1997). $20.

When Your Wife Says No: Forced Sex in Marriage by Fay Honey Knopp (1994). $7.

Protocol for Phallometric Assessment: A Clinician's Guide by Deloris T. Roys & Pat Roys (1999). $10.

Personal Sentence Completion Inventory by L.C. Miccio-Fonseca, PhD (1998). $65, includes ten inventories and user's guide. Additional inventories available in packs of 25 for $31.25.

What's Happening in Our Family? Understanding Sexual Abuse through Metaphors by Connie Ostis, Ph.D. LCSW (2002) $20.

But He Says He Loves Me: girls Speak Out on Dating Abuse by Nicole B. Sperekas, Ph.D. (2001) $15.

The Safer Society Press is part of The Safer Society Foundation, Inc., a 501(c)3 nonprofit national agency dedicated to the prevention and treatment of sexual abuse. We publish additional books, audiocassetttes, and training videos related to the treatment of sexual abuse. To receive a catalog of our complete listings, please check the box on the order form (next page) and mail it to the address listed or call us at (802) 247- 3132. For more information on the Safer Society Foundation, Inc., visit our website at http://www.safersociety.org.

Order Form

Date: _____

All books shipped via United Parcel Service. Please include a street location for shipping as we cannot ship to a Post Office box address.

Shipping Address:

Name and/or Agency _____

Street Address (no PO boxes) _____

_____

City _____ State _____ Zip _____

Billing Address (if different from shipping address):

Address _____

_____

City _____ State _____ Zip _____

Daytime phone (_____) _____

P.O. # _____

Visa or MasterCard # _____

Exp. Date _____

Signature (FOR CREDIT CARD ORDER) _____

☐ Please send a catalog.   ☐ Do not add me to your mailing list.

QTY	TITLE	UNIT PRICE	TOTAL COST

	Sub Total	
	VT residents (only) add sales tax	
	Shipping (see below)	
	TOTAL	

All orders must be prepaid.
Make checks payable to
and mail to:

Safer Society Press
PO BOX 340
BRANDON, VT 05733-0340
www.safersociety.org

All prices subject to change
without notice. No Returns.
Bulk discounts available, please inquire.
Call for quote on rush orders.

Shipping & Handling
1-4 items - $8   26-30 items - $23
5-10 items - $11   31-35 items - $26
11-15 items - $15   36-40 items - $29
16-20 items - $17   41-50 items - $34
21-25 items - $20   51+ items call for quote

Phone orders accepted with
MasterCard or Visa. Call (802) 247-3132.